# One Step at a Time: A Vietnamese Child Finds Her Way

Marsha Forchuk Skrypuch

# One Step at a Time

## A Vietnamese Child Finds Her Way

pajamapress

The publisher gratefully acknowledges the support of the Canada Council for the Arts and the Ontario Arts
Council for its publishing program. We acknowledge the financial support of the Government of Canada through
the Canada Book Fund (CBF) for our publishing activities.

Library and Archives Canada Cataloguing in Publication

Skrypuch, Marsha Forchuk, 1954-
        One step at a time : a Vietnamese child finds her
way / Marsha Forchuk Skrypuch.

Issued also in electronic format.
ISBN 978-1-927485-01-9 (bound).

        1. Son Thi Anh, Tuyet--Juvenile literature. 2. Children
with disabilities--Hospital care--Canada. 3. Immigrant children--
Vietnam--Juvenile literature. 4. Immigrant children--Canada--
Juvenile literature. 5. Courage--Juvenile literature. I. Title.

RJ138.S57 2012          618.927          C2012-903427-4

U.S. Publisher Cataloging-in-Publication Data (U.S.)

Skrypuch, Marsha Forchuk, 1954-.
    One step at a time : a Vietnamese child finds her way / Marsha Forchuk Skrypuch.
[ ] p. : ill. ;  cm.
Summary: Vietnamese-born Tuyet has escaped her war-torn homeland and found a loving family in Canada,
but her dreams of running and playing with her adopted siblings, are hampered by her clubfoot and leg
weakened by polio.
ISBN-13: 978-1-927485-01-9

1. Son Thi Anh, Tuyet – Juvenile literature.   2. Children with disabilities – Biography – Juvenile literature.
3. Adopted children – Canada – Biography – Juvenile literature. 4. Vietnamese Canadians – Biography –
Juvenile literature.  I. Title.
959.704/3086914092 [B] dc23   DS559.8C53.S5797   2012

Cover and book design–Rebecca Buchanan
Manufactured by Friesens in Altona, Manitoba, Canada in 2012.

Pajama Press Inc.                          Distributed in the U.S. by Orca Book Publishers
469 Richmond St E, Toronto Ontario, Canada    PO Box 468  Custer, WA, 98240-0468, USA
www.pajamapress.ca

# Photo Credits

To Beth, Lara, and Aaron

# Table of Contents

# Chapter One

# The Night Before

Tuyet burrowed into her nest of pillows and covers on the throw rug between Beth and Lara's beds. She had a room of her own, but Tuyet still found comfort in the sound of her new sisters' rhythmic breathing. Her mom and dad had decided it would be all right to sleep on the floor, at least until she was ready to sleep on her own.

If she was very still, she could hear the tick-tick of a clock down the hallway, along with Dad's heavy snores. She kept her eyes tightly closed and hugged her Holly Hobbie doll, but sleep would not come. In just a few hours, Tuyet's life would change forever.

Instead of sleep, the memories came…

*A giant* BOOM…*fire and smoke.*

*Pain.*

*Her back and scalp on fire. Hair aflame and smoking.*

*Doctors hovering over her with strange instruments.*

*The* whup whup whup *of helicopters above.*

*Moans from other injured people in cots close by...*

Tuyet thought she had buried those memories for good. But ever since her ankle surgery had been scheduled, the terrors were back, keeping her awake nearly every night. She pulled the covers over her head and squeezed her eyes shut. The images wouldn't go away. Still clutching her doll, Tuyet pushed off the covers and sat up. Four-year-old Beth and three-year-old Lara were sleeping peacefully.

Tuyet balanced on her one good foot and peeked though the curtains at the night sky.

No helicopters, no fire, no smoke.

This wasn't the orphanage in Saigon. She didn't live in Vietnam anymore.

Tuyet left the curtain open, just enough to let the moonlight in. She looked down at her legs. The right one was strong and straight, and her foot pointed in the right direction. But her left leg was no larger than Lara's, and it was weak. Her ankle turned inward, making her foot useless. She had to limp on the bone of her ankle to get around. She'd push on her knee with the palm of her hand to make her injured leg move. She'd gotten used to the build-up of calluses on her knee and hand, and she hardly noticed the constant pain in her ankle anymore.

What would her left leg and ankle look like after the surgery? It was hard to imagine.

How much would the surgery hurt? That's what frightened her the most. She could handle the pain she already had, but she did not want more of it.

Tuyet tugged the curtains closed then limped to the bedroom door and opened it, listening for the sound of Dad's snores. His snoring was usually a comfort, but tonight it wasn't enough.

Tuyet held her doll in the crook of her arm as she silently shuffled down the hallway, first poking her head into Aaron's room. He was safe in his crib. When she reached her parents' bedroom, Tuyet pushed open the door. They were in bed, bathed in shadows, fast asleep.

How she longed to crawl under the covers between them. Maybe the memories would stay away. But she didn't want to bother them. She got down onto the floor and pulled herself under their bed, huddling into a ball with her doll safe within her arms, little bits of dust tickling her nose. The space beneath the bed was just the perfect size for her. Dad's snoring was comfortingly loud.

Tuyet fell into a dreamless sleep.

In the morning, beams of sunlight woke her as they lit the floor around her parents' bed. She pulled herself out from under the bed and shuffled quietly back to her own spot between her two sisters. She closed her eyes and pretended to sleep, pleased at the thought of the secret safe place she had found to keep the memories away. If only she could stay there forever. If only she didn't have to go to the hospital today.

Beth and Lara woke, but Tuyet kept her eyes closed. She could feel a warm hand on her shoulder. "Wake up, Sis," said Lara. "It's your operation day."

Tuyet squeezed her eyes shut. Maybe if she pretended to be asleep, she wouldn't have to go.

She heard her sisters leave the bedroom, then heard morning noises down the hallway. Dad came in and knelt beside her.

"Time to get up, Tuyet."

She kept her eyes closed tight.

Mom's footsteps stopped at the doorway. "Why don't we let her sleep a bit longer, John?"

Tuyet didn't understand all the words, but whatever Mom said, it worked. Dad got up and left. A little while later, she heard the car pull out of the driveway. Maybe he decided not to take her to the hospital after all.

But an hour later, Dad came back. "It's time for us to go."

1-1        *The Morris family. From left, Lara, John, Tuyet, Beth, Dorothy, Aaron*

## Chapter Two

## Red Shoes

Tuyet sat in the front seat of the car with her doll on her lap and Dad in the driver's seat. Beth and Lara solemnly waved good-bye from the front window of the house. Aaron stood between them, his two hands firmly planted on the glass.

Mom crouched beside the open door of the car so that she was eye level with Tuyet. "You are my brave girl," she said, lightly kissing Tuyet on the cheek.

Mom closed the car door.

Dad turned on the ignition and put the car in reverse. "You are going to be okay," he said.

Tuyet didn't know the meaning of the words, but they sounded reassuring. What was about to happen was still unknown, but right now she cherished what she had—her own mom and dad, two sisters and a brother, a home of her own. No matter what happened about her ankle, she had her own family and her own home. That was what she cared about most.

As they drove in silence, Tuyet looked down at her special pair of red shoes. Just the sight of them reassured Tuyet that she was loved. Tuyet smiled to herself, remembering.

When she had met her family for the first time, she had been wearing rain boots. Tuyet could barely walk in the white boots, which were many sizes too large. But it was raining outside, and the care workers couldn't find anything else for her to wear. She couldn't leave the building in Toronto barefoot.

Everyone else in the Morris family had a pair of shoes. Even Aaron, who was still a baby, had shoes! Beth's favorite shoes were beautiful shiny red ones with a strap across the top. Tuyet loved gliding her finger over their smooth, glossy surfaces. Lara's favorites were bright pink running shoes. Not only were they pretty, but they had tough, rubbery soles that were perfect for running and kicking a ball. Tuyet longed to run and kick a ball. She could barely walk in the big white boots. But she knew that even if she had shoes like everybody else, she still wouldn't be able to kick a ball. She'd need two good feet inside the shoes to be able to do that.

Mom knew that Tuyet wanted shoes of her own instead of the ugly white boots. Tuyet had only been in Brantford for a couple of days when Mom took her shoe shopping at the huge Woolco store. Tuyet looked at the racks and racks of shoes in every imaginable style and every possible size. She couldn't believe that stores could be so big. Tuyet limped through the aisles, wishing she could wear a pair of shoes like other people. Mom followed behind, her brow knitted in thought.

Tuyet picked out a pair of red shiny shoes. They were just like Beth's.

Mom held onto the shoes, but they kept on looking. Suddenly, Mom's eyes lit up. She grabbed something from a rack above Tuyet's eye level and then motioned for Tuyet to sit in a chair.

Mom knelt down and drew off the ugly rubber boots. Onto the right foot, she slipped a red shoe. She pulled the strap tight across the top of Tuyet's foot and fastened the buckle.

Tuyet straightened out her good knee and admired her healthy foot. The shoe looked beautiful from every angle. If only the matching shoe would fit onto her tiny left foot with the bent ankle, but of course she knew that wasn't possible.

She smiled at Mom to hide the heaviness in her heart. She knew how hard Mom was trying, and that in itself felt good.

Mom grinned mischievously and showed Tuyet the other item. It was red as well, but it looked like a small sweater. Mom gently drew off the other rubber boot and carefully pulled the red knitted thing over Tuyet's tiny foot, making sure not to hurt her bent ankle, drawing it up to her calf.

Once it was on, Tuyet realized that it wasn't a sweater, but a soft slipper with a sturdy leather sole. She looked down at both of her feet and nearly wept. For the first time in her life, she owned a pair of shoes, and they were red, too!

Dad went over a bump in the road and Tuyet's thoughts about that shopping trip fled from her mind. She remembered that she was on the way to the hospital. She was going to have surgery. She looked back down at her special red shoes. That made her feel better.

Tuyet gazed out the window and realized that they were already on the highway. She watched Dad as he concentrated on the road. He turned to her briefly and smiled.

"It's going to be fine," he said.

Tuyet thought back to the day she first found out she was going to have surgery. It had been only a few days after Mom had bought her the shoes.

Mom wouldn't let her help with the chores and wouldn't let her help with Aaron.

"Scoot," said Mom. "Go play."

Tuyet tried hard at this new skill, this *playing*, which seemed so important to her parents. She and her sisters and brother would play on the swing set in the backyard, and they would make mounds in the sandbox. And that was fun. But sometimes Tuyet would sit on the front step. Most of the children on the street were young like her sisters and brother, but there were two boys her age next door, and sometimes they'd kick a ball back and forth to each other. She was sure they didn't even know that she existed. How she longed to play with them, to kick a ball. But even with her new shoes, Tuyet could not kick a ball. She could not run.

So just as she had done in the Saigon orphanage, Tuyet sat and watched instead.

One evening, Tuyet was sitting on the front lawn when an unfamiliar car pulled into the Morris driveway. A Vietnamese woman stepped out. Tuyet began to shake as she struggled to her feet. Was the woman here to take Tuyet away?

"Good afternoon, Son Thi Anh Tuyet," the woman said in Vietnamese. "My name is Mrs. Nguyen. I am here to visit your parents. Can you let them know that I am here?"

"Go away!" Tuyet shouted in Vietnamese. She expected the woman to be angered by her rudeness, but the woman's face remained serene.

Mrs. Nguyen walked up to the front door and knocked.

In a panic, Tuyet limped away as fast as she could. Looking for a place to hide, she crept behind a bush in the neighbor's yard.

Then she peeked through the branches. Mom had opened the door.

"Please make her go," Tuyet prayed.

But Mom was smiling! The woman followed Mom into the house.

Tuyet waited behind the bush, her heart sinking.

Was there something she had done to anger Mom and Dad?

Tuyet had been so sure that she was part of the Morris family now. Mom wouldn't have bought her the special red shoes unless she was family, so why was this woman here? Tuyet did not want to go back to the orphanage. She was a Morris now. This was home.

Dad opened the front door and stepped out. "Tuyet!" he called. "Where are you?"

Tuyet crouched down.

It didn't take Dad long to find her. He picked her up gently and carried her inside. Tuyet was numb with fear.

He sat down on the sofa beside Mom, his arms still wrapped protectively around Tuyet's waist.

"Child, I am here to help you," said Mrs. Nguyen in Vietnamese.

Tuyet buried her head into her father's chest. She could feel Mom's hand caressing her shoulder.

"Your parents asked me to translate some things for them."

Tuyet did not want a translation. She could not stop trembling.

Dad hugged her more tightly.

Mom said, "We love you, Tuyet. Everything will be fine."

"Most important," said Mrs. Nguyen. "You are not going back to Vietnam."

Tuyet held her herself very still. Had she heard right?

"This is your home. These are your parents. That will not change."

Tuyet loosened her grip on Dad's neck and turned her head so she could see Mrs. Nguyen from the corner of her eye. The woman seemed calm and kind. She did not look like a liar.

Tuyet slipped off Dad's lap and snuggled in to the narrow spot on the sofa between Mom and Dad. Mom grabbed one of her hands and gave it a reassuring squeeze. Dad held her other hand in both of his.

"You want to be able to play like other children, don't you?" asked Mrs. Nguyen.

It was as if Mrs. Nguyen had reached inside Tuyet's heart. More than anything, this is what Tuyet wanted, but she knew it was not possible. She looked down at her shoes. She couldn't answer Mrs. Nguyen.

"Your parents need to take you to the doctor, to see what can be done to strengthen and straighten your left ankle."

"I don't want a doctor," said Tuyet.

"You need a doctor," said the woman.

"A doctor will cut open my ankle."

"Only to put it back together in a better way. Don't you want to try, Son Thi Anh Tuyet?"

"Will I be able to walk?" asked Tuyet.

"Maybe," said Mrs. Nguyen.

"Will I be able to kick a ball?"

"One step at a time," said Mrs. Nguyen with a smile.

This plan to have her ankle straightened felt like reaching for the stars. Tuyet had been eager when the surgery seemed like a dream in the future, but now that the day was upon her, she was having second thoughts.

Stars weren't meant to be touched. Maybe her ankle was never meant to be straight.

Tuyet looked out the car window and tried not to think.

3-1                                           *McMaster University Medical Centre,*
*opened in 1972*

# Chapter Three

## The Hospital

Dad parked the car. He carried Tuyet into the huge concrete building.

Tuyet tried to calm herself. She thought of the frightening experiences that had transformed her life.

The nuns at the orphanage. They had terrified her at first, but they protected her from the bombs and bullets and they gave her food and a place to sleep.

The giant airplane. Tuyet had covered her eyes at the sight of it. But she made herself go inside, and that huge flying building rescued her from the war. If she hadn't swallowed her fear, she might never have come to Canada.

She might never have found her new family...

Tuyet clutched her father's neck with one arm and held her doll in the other as he carried her through the busy corridors of McMaster Hospital. She watched a woman pass by with a boy who was about her own age. They didn't notice her at all.

The boy did not look scared. If anything, he looked bored.

Tuyet looked at the faces of other people.

No one looked frightened.

Maybe this hospital really would straighten her ankle. Tuyet tried to appear calm as she and Dad got into the elevator. Dad pressed the number Three.

Three was not an unlucky number.

The doors opened up onto the brightly painted children's ward, with its floor-to-ceiling windows, but Tuyet was too numb to take in the details.

She didn't notice the playroom filled with child-sized furniture and boxes of toys, or the cartoon mural on the wall, or the huge see-through fish tank.

Tuyet thought they would let Dad stay with her, but instead they sent him home.

Tuyet trembled as a uniformed woman helped her remove her special red shoes and her socks. The nurse took away Tuyet's doll and helped her change into a plain cotton gown. The woman neatly folded Tuyet's bell-bottomed pants and new top that Mom had bought her. Then she lifted her onto a wheeled cot and motioned for Tuyet to lie down.

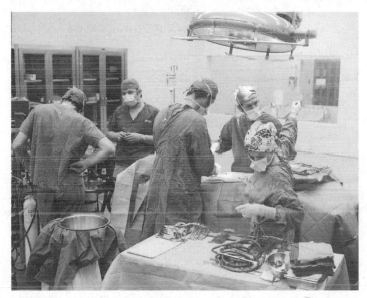

3-2                         *McMaster University Medical Centre*
*operating room, circa 1975*

Tuyet felt so alone. So afraid.

She tried not to think of anything at all as a smiling man wheeled her into a stark white room with lots of shiny metal instruments and bright lights.

People with cotton masks over the bottom part of

their faces gathered around her and spoke in soothing tones.

Tuyet willed herself not to think of that other time in the hospital. *People weeping, helicopters overhead.* This would be different. This time she would have a family to go home to.

Warm hands steadied her forearm and she felt a faint prick, then a sensation of cold tingling under her skin. Her eyes went heavy.

A flash of memory—

*She is lying on a sweat-drenched mat on the floor of a bamboo stilt house. Helicopters fly overhead, while the* bang *and* crash *of explosions make the ground tremble.*

*A woman hovers over her, cooling her forehead with a damp cloth, but it doesn't help. Pain spasms through her left leg. The woman holds a cup to her mouth, but the water dribbles down her chin.*

*Her throat is parched but she cannot swallow…*

*She hovers between wake and sleep.*

*She lies in the stilt house for days. The woman is always there, her eyes red from weeping. "I cannot help you, my daughter. Please do not die."*

*She is wracked with pain.*

*Strong sinewy arms lift her from the sweat-soaked mat. Her mother runs, carrying her, as bombs explode all round.*

*Another cot and other doctors. The spasms go away from her left leg, but she cannot get it to move anymore. Doctors send her weeping mother home.*

*A strange veiled woman in white carries Tuyet away from the hospital...to a building with many other children. Tuyet calls for her mother. She grows hoarse from crying.*

*Then she forgets.*

*Much later a woman visits. Is it her mother?*

*She visits once.*

*Twice.*

*Never again.*

Tuyet shook the images out of her mind. That was in the past. It was a time of deep sadness. A time of belonging to no one. A time that she needed to forget.

Tuyet's tongue felt swollen and her throat was dry, but she felt no pain. This was strange in itself. Tuyet could not remember a time without pain. Didn't everyone feel constant pain? It was just a part of living, after all.

She opened one eye and saw that she was no longer in the operating room. Instead she was propped up in a bed with rails along both sides. She opened her other eye. Holly Hobbie was tucked in beside her. Tuyet smiled. The doll reminded her of home, that she was Tuyet Morris now.

When she reached to hug her doll, something pulled at her left hand. A length of narrow plastic tubing was attached to the back of her hand with a bandage. Her eyes followed the length of tube to the other end, where it was attached to a clear plastic bag filled with fluid. The bag was hooked onto a tall metal pole. Fluid drip-dripped steadily from the plastic bag into the tubing.

A kind-looking woman wearing a flowered smock sat in a chair close to Tuyet's bed. She offered Tuyet a plastic glass with a straw and said something in English. Tuyet took a sip—fresh cold water—and was reassured to find that she could swallow it. The water felt so soothing on her tongue and throat that she would have drunk the whole glass, but the woman took it away from her after just two sips.

Tuyet looked down the length of the bed. The outline

of both her legs was visible through the white cotton sheet. Her left leg, usually smaller, looked bigger now, and it was propped on a pillow. She reached out to touch it.

It felt like a rock.

She pulled back the sheet. From just below her knee to the tip of her toe, her leg was encased in what looked like a column of white cement. Even though there was nothing in her stomach except for those little sips of water, Tuyet felt as if she was about to throw up. She lay back against her pillow.

How would she ever be able to walk with this huge piece of cement weighing her down? Maybe it was all a nightmare. She closed her eyes and tried to make it go away.

# Chapter Four

# Black Button

Tuyet drifted in and out of sleep. Once, when she was barely awake, the woman in the flowered smock showed her a black button on the end of a long cord.

"If you need me, push this," she said, looping it securely around the bed rail.

Tuyet wished she knew what the woman was saying.

Another time, the woman woke her and helped her sit up. Tuyet felt dizzy and her head was heavy with sleep, but the woman gently helped Tuyet off the bed and guided her to the bathroom. Once Tuyet was finished and back in bed, the woman pointed to the button again.

"Push this if you need me."

And then Tuyet understood. If she needed to go to

the bathroom, she should push the button and the woman would come back to assist her.

It was still dark outside, too early to be awake. Tuyet closed her eyes, but it was no use. She was wide awake. She closed her eyes again and tried to pretend that she was snuggled in her nest of pillows and blankets on the floor between Beth and Lara. But her spine sank down into the unfamiliar hospital mattress. She tried to shift her position, but the tubing in the back of her hand got in the way whenever she moved, and the cast was heavy and awkward. She tried to think of home, but the sounds were all wrong. Instead of Dad's snore, she could hear people speaking in low voices down the hallway and a faint *beep, beep, beep* of a machine in another room. No matter how hard she tried, she couldn't trick herself into feeling at home…but then…

*She is back inside the giant airplane that will carry her away from Vietnam. The caregivers are frantic; they bring in more babies. Rows of cardboard boxes, all filled with hot, screaming babies. Sweat drips down her forehead and stings her eyes as she moves from box to box.*

*Her hand trembles as she reaches into a box to comfort a frightened infant.*

*"Soon you will be safe," she coos, hoping it isn't a lie.*

*A woman scoops Tuyet off the floor of the aircraft and sets her in a chair. She reaches for a seatbelt, but instead the woman pours wet cement on both of Tuyet's legs. It hardens in an instant. She cannot move.*

*She peers out the window of the airplane. Beth and Lara are on the tarmac, and their legs are in cement as well. Aaron sits on the hot pavement between them, screaming. He sounds just like the babies in the boxes.*

*Soon the airplane will be taking off. She has to warn them. If they don't get on the airplane, they will be left behind. She will never see them again!*

*Tuyet pounds on the window, but Beth and Lara don't see her. They are looking down at their cement legs—*

Tuyet woke with a jolt. She looked around and saw that she was not on the airplane. She was in a hospital bed and only one leg had cement on it. Beth, Aaron, and Lara were safe at home, not in Vietnam. Tuyet knew it, but her heart was still pounding.

Her ankle throbbed and her bum felt tingly from lying in the same spot for so long. She tried shifting her weight, but it was impossible to get comfortable. She reached down to massage her ankle, but with the cast on, she couldn't get to the spot where it hurt.

Tuyet flopped back on her pillow, feeling trapped and frustrated. Hot tears spilled down her cheeks, which made her angry with herself. She took a deep breath and willed the pain away. But it was no use.

The whole thing was a big mistake. Had the doctors cut her leg open as they said they would, things would have been bad enough. But instead they had just covered her leg in cement. Before they started fooling around with her leg, at least she had been able to get around. Now she was trapped in this cast, and her leg hurt more than ever before. She should have been satisfied with what she already had instead of trying to reach for the stars.

She drifted off to sleep again, but stabbing pains woke her up. The pain would have been bearable with Dad and Mom there, but Tuyet was all alone. She tried to hold her feelings in, but still the tears coursed down her cheeks.

Desperate, Tuyet pushed the black button. She

didn't have to go to the bathroom, but she needed to have someone close by.

A nurse rushed in. It wasn't the woman in the flowered smock. "What can I get you?" she asked.

Tuyet didn't want the nurse to see her cry. She turned her face to the pillow. The nurse sat down on the edge of the bed and murmured words in English in a soothing voice. It felt better to have someone there with her, even if it was a stranger, and even if she had no idea what the woman was saying. Tuyet closed her eyes and tried to think of nothing.

After hours of drifting between troubled sleep and painful wakings, Tuyet was glad when night finally ended, and early morning light poured through the window. Now maybe Mom or Dad would come to take her home. She could hear carts wheeling up and down the hallway and the voices of men and women. But no one sounded familiar.

A woman, another stranger, entered the room carrying a tray of food. She set it down on a rolling table and propped Tuyet into a sitting position. All the while she chatted away to Tuyet in English.

Tuyet looked at the food on the tray. A glass of apple

juice, a cup of green Jell-O, a bowl of brown broth. It didn't look like very much. A dull ache in the pit of her stomach reminded Tuyet that she was hungry, but she did not feel like eating. Her ankle wasn't the only thing screaming with pain. Now her knee, forced into an unnatural position by the cast, began to throb. She pushed the food away and closed her eyes. The woman said something in English, but Tuyet just hung her head.

Some time later, yet another uniformed woman came in. Tuyet was having trouble keeping track of them all. This one listened to Tuyet's heart and checked the fluid in the plastic bag on the pole. She frowned as she read notes from the clipboard she took from the end of Tuyet's bed.

She asked Tuyet a question in English. Tuyet shook her head. Couldn't they all just leave her alone?

In careful, slow English, Tuyet said, "I want Mom and Dad."

"Can't you see she's in pain?"

Tuyet's eyes flew open. Dad stood there, hands on hips, a shocked look on his face. A nurse hurried out the door.

He sounded angry with the hospital people. Maybe

he and Mom hadn't realized what would be happening to her leg either. They had been told she'd be getting her ankle straightened, not a leg dipped in cement.

Mom sat on the edge of Tuyet's bed and leaned in, kissing her on the top of her head. Tuyet got a dusky floral whiff of Mom's favorite perfume. It smelled like—

"Home," pleaded Tuyet.

"Soon," said Mom, gently brushing a stray lock of hair behind Tuyet's ear.

The nurse came back, holding a hypodermic needle. Tuyet shook her head.

"For the pain," said Dad.

The nurse swabbed a spot on Tuyet's butt with a bit of cold, wet cotton. A small pinch, then warmth. Within seconds, Tuyet felt the pain ebbing away from her knee and ankle. She lay back against her pillow and sighed. It felt so wonderful to be free of the pain. How did Dad know she was hurting? She hadn't told him. How did he know what would help? It had never occurred to Tuyet to tell anyone about the pain. She'd never dreamed they'd be interested.

Mom held up the button that was attached to the cord. She pretended to push it, then pointed to the nurse, who was still holding the empty needle.

Now Tuyet understood! The button was for help. *All* kinds of help. Tuyet still wanted to go home, but she didn't feel quite so trapped now that she knew the nurses could make the pain go away. All she had to do was figure out a way to let them know what she needed.

Dad came to visit the following day. He examined her face carefully for signs of pain. Tuyet grinned at him. There was no pain. Dad's face broke out into a broad smile. He sat down on the bed and gave her a gentle hug. Tuyet clung to him, wishing she never had to let go.

After a few minutes, Dad unwrapped her arms from his neck and said something in English.

A young Vietnamese man stepped into the room and stood at the foot of her bed.

"Good day, Son Thi Anh Tuyet," he said in Vietnamese. "My name is Hoang Tuy. I am a student at this hospital."

Tuyet understood immediately that this man had come to help her. She thought back to how rude she had been when she first met Mrs. Nguyen. She wouldn't embarrass herself like that again. She sat up as straight as she could in her bed and bowed her head respectfully, in the traditional way.

Tuy returned Tuyet's greeting with a slight bow of his own. "Your father has asked me to explain what is happening to you."

"Thank you, Honorable Mr. Hoang," said Tuyet in Vietnamese.

"The cast on your leg," said Tuy, "has to stay on for six weeks."

"Honorable sir, will I need to stay in the hospital all that time?"

"No. You'll be here for a few more days and then you will go home."

"Mr. Hoang, why did they put this cement on my leg?" asked Tuyet. "I thought they were going to cut my ankle open."

"They did," said Tuy. "Your ankle has had surgery, and your foot is now straight. The cast is there to give your ankle some time to rest and heal."

"And in six weeks the cast comes off?"

Tuy nodded. "This week, the people at the hospital will show you how to walk with crutches. You'll be home before you know it."

"Thank you, Mr. Hoang," said Tuyet, bowing her head again. "It was kind of you to tell me this."

"If you would like, I could drop in later this week, to see how you are doing," said Tuy.

Tuyet smiled. "That would be kind of you, sir."

Tuy took one step toward the door, but Dad held up his hand. They spoke in English for a few minutes. Tuy left, but came back a few moments later with a pad of paper and a pen. He frowned in concentration as he wrote.

He tore off the top sheet and gave it to Tuyet. "Push your button when you need something," he said. "Once the nurse gets here, use this paper to point to the English words for what you need."

Tuyet looked at what he'd written. In one column were phrases in Vietnamese—*leg hurts, bathroom, hungry, thirsty, play*. Beside each Vietnamese phrase was a corresponding phrase in English.

Tuyet folded the paper carefully and held it to her chest. "Thank you, Mr. Hoang," she said, grinning. "This will help me very much."

# Chapter Five

## Home Again

The week went by slowly. Tuyet learned how to get around on crutches. The woman with the floral smock visited her every day, and she urged Tuyet to follow her to the playroom to be with the other children.

Tuyet preferred to stay in her room. Although she gathered up the courage to walk carefully down to the playroom, she stood by the doorway and watched the other children play, too shy to join in. None of them had almond eyes and golden skin like her. No one else had a leg in cement, or even crutches. It was hard to see why some of them needed to be in the hospital at all.

Mostly Tuyet played by herself or stared at the fish in the aquarium as she waited for the woman to usher her back to her room. No matter how kind the staff was or how interesting the toys were, Tuyet could not overcome her shyness. She longed to go home, to be with her family.

Sometimes at night, the nightmare would come back. It always seemed to be about the airplane, but other parts of it changed. In one dream, Tuyet was alone on the Hercules, searching frantically through boxes and storage areas, calling for Lara, Beth, Aaron, Mom, and Dad. Another time, she stood on the pavement in the sweltering heat and watched the airplane take off, her family pounding at the windows, trying to get out.

Dad came at visiting hour every day, but he never brought Aaron, Beth, or Lara with him. Children weren't allowed to visit. And most days Mom had to stay home to look after the children while Dad was at the hospital.

Finally, the day arrived.

Tuyet dressed in a pink striped shirt and a pair of wide bell-bottoms, which fit over her cast. She wore her one red shoe, and she stretched the red knit slipper over the foot of her cast. She wanted to walk out of the hospital on her own two legs and her crutches, but the staff insisted she leave in a wheelchair. Dad left a few minutes before she did because he had to get the car from the parking lot.

When the nurse pushed Tuyet's wheelchair into the elevator, Tuyet was surprised to see an adult with two good legs being pushed in a wheelchair as well. That made her feel better. They weren't making her take the wheelchair because of her leg; they made everyone leave that way.

Tuyet's heart filled with joy when the outside doors glided open and there was Dad, leaning against the car and smiling from ear to ear. Four ribbons were wrapped securely around his hand, and bobbing above his head, attached to the ribbons, were four big round balls—a red, a yellow, a pink, and a blue.

Dad gently lifted her from the wheelchair and lowered her into the back so that her cast was lying across the seat. He tucked a pillow against the small of her back so she wasn't leaning directly on the door. Once she was settled, he sat down on the edge of the back seat and carefully unwound the ribbons from his hand.

"These are for you, Tuyet," he said, wrapping the ribbons around her hand.

She giggled as her father struggled to get the bobbing

balls to stay inside the car. He shoved the last one in and closed the back door, then climbed into the driver's seat. He grinned and pointed to the balls. "*Balloons.*"

Tuyet watched the balloons tap gently against the roof of the car as they drove along the highway. It felt so good to be almost home.

When they pulled into the driveway, Beth ran outside to greet her, with Lara close behind. Mom followed with Aaron on her hip. The sight of her family together filled Tuyet with joy. This was all she'd ever wanted. A family of her own. A family to love.

Beth opened the back door of the car and Lara reached in, tugging on Tuyet's bell-bottoms. Tuyet slid gingerly forward until the foot of her cast touched the surface of the driveway. She carefully unwrapped the ribbons from around her hand. She separated out the yellow balloon and tied the ribbon around Lara's wrist. She gave the pink one to Beth and tied the red one to Aaron's arm. She kept the blue one for herself. It was exciting to have something to give her brother and sisters.

"Let me help you, sis," said Beth, her pink balloon pulling at her wrist. She wrapped both hands around one of Tuyet's.

But Tuyet shook her head. "Crutches?"

Dad got them from the trunk and steadied them in place so Tuyet could pull herself up to a standing position. Slowly, carefully, she walked across the driveway. It was more difficult to maneuver her cast on the driveway; it wasn't smooth like the hospital floors. The walkway was smoother than the driveway, but it was still hard work. Beth ran ahead of her and held open the door. Tuyet was proud of herself as she stepped through the front door.

But then she stopped. How would she manage to get up the six carpeted steps that led to the living room? She thought of how easy it had been to get up and down these steps before the surgery. In fact, she had never given these steps much thought before.

"I can carry you up to the top," said Dad, making a lifting motion with his arms.

Tuyet shook her head.

This was something Tuyet had to do on her own, but she did let Dad hold her blue balloon. She gingerly placed the rubber bottoms of her crutches on the lowest step and held them steady. She stepped onto the lowest stair with her good foot, then struggled to pull up her cement-encased leg to the same level. For one dizzy moment, she thought she was going to fall off, but Dad stood behind her, ready to catch her.

Tuyet looked up. Mom stood at the top, smiling encouragingly. Beth and Lara had scrambled up the stairs and were now sitting cross-legged on the shag carpeting on the living-room level, their balloons floating above their heads. Aaron sat cuddled between them.

"You can do it, sis!" said Beth.

Tuyet looked up at her siblings and smiled.

One step at a time.

Her face was covered with sweat by the time she got up to the living-room level. It took her a moment to catch her breath.

She surveyed the room, expecting it to look as it had before she'd gone to the hospital. But now the sofa had been made into a daybed, with a new pillow and blanket.

"For you," said Mom.

Leaning heavily on her crutches Tuyet managed to get over to the sofa, and then nearly fell into it. What a wonderful, cozy place! From her daybed, Tuyet could look out the front window. She could see through to the kitchen too. There was a television in the kitchen, and

Mom had turned it toward the living room so that Tuyet could see it from her spot on the sofa. Tuyet was thrilled. She would be in the center of the family circle.

On that first night home, Tuyet had expected to sleep in her cozy spot on the floor between Beth and Lara's beds, but when she hobbled into her sisters' bedroom, she was shocked to see only the rug between the two beds.

Beth motioned for her to come and see the other room—the bedroom where she had spent her first night. Tuyet stepped in through the doorway of that other room. The bed was made up. The window was open a crack and a cool fresh breeze blew in through the curtains.

Tuyet pasted a smile on her face, but her heart ached with disappointment.

At the hospital, she'd had to sleep in a room all by herself and she'd hated it. All week, she had longed to be home, to be surrounded by her family. Why couldn't she sleep in her cozy nest on the floor between her sisters?

Tuyet tried hard to look happy as she played at the kitchen table with her sisters all afternoon, and she was thrilled when Mom cooked chicken and rice for dinner, and served sweet, fresh pineapple for dessert. It tasted so much better than the hospital food. But when bedtime loomed, try as she might, Tuyet couldn't keep the heaviness from her heart.

Once she and her siblings finished brushing their teeth, Tuyet stumped down the hall to Beth and Lara's room. Dad stood in the doorway while Tuyet pointed to the empty spot between their beds.

"Tuyet sleep?" she said.

Dad pointed to the cast on her leg. "You can't sleep on the floor anymore, my dear daughter," he said. "You could hurt yourself."

Tuyet's eyes filled with tears, but Dad just shook his head. Tuyet slowly made her way to her own bedroom.

Mom sat on the bed with Holly Hobbie on her lap. Tuyet changed into her pajamas and leaned her crutches up against the wall within easy reach of the bed. She slipped under the covers with her doll. Then Mom and Dad tucked her in and kissed her good night.

Mom turned off the main light in Tuyet's room, but it wasn't completely dark. Tuyet could see the shape of her dresser, the outline of the window, and the curtains fluttering gently. She thought of her sisters in the room next to her and longed to be with them.

Tuyet hugged her doll and tried to sleep. This bed seemed more comfortable than she remembered. In fact, it was a lot more comfortable than the hospital bed. She reached over with one hand and felt the cool wood of one crutch. She could go into her sisters' room anytime she wanted. But for now, she'd rest her eyes, in this soft and cozy bed.

Before she knew it, she was sound asleep.

In the morning, she woke up feeling happy and loved. Tuyet smiled to herself at the thought of it. Now that she had a family, she didn't have to worry about being in the exact same room with them all of the time. They were all the same family and they were a part of her. Tuyet was home.

5-1                                        *The Morris family home, circa 1975*

# Chapter Six

# Brady Bunch

As the days went by, Tuyet became adept at getting around on her crutches. Inside the cast, her leg itched like crazy. She longed to be able to scratch her ankle, but at least itchy skin was better than pain. Maybe the itching was a sign of healing.

Tuyet had counted out on the kitchen calendar the forty-two days that she'd have her cast on. June eighteenth was the day it was to come off.

The days settled into a routine. She played with Beth, Lara, and Aaron in the sandbox when the weather was nice. Beth and Lara would point to things and tell her the English names. Tuyet would repeat after them, "Shovel, pail, sandbox…swing." She tried to play on the swing too, but it took all her concentration just to sit on the seat and balance herself with her cement-encased foot planted firmly on the ground.

When she was too tired to sit outside, she would sit on the daybed and look out the front window at the older boys who lived next door. She longed to be able to run and kick and play as they did.

Mom liked to watch soap operas on the television when Aaron took his afternoon nap. Tuyet would color quietly or flip through books with Beth and Lara, who would point at pictures and tell her the English words.

After the soap operas were over, the sisters could choose what to watch. Tuyet had not paid much attention to the television before her surgery. She had preferred to play outside as much as possible. Now that she was forced to rest her leg, the stories on TV broke up the monotony of her day. Tuyet's favorite show was *The Brady Bunch*, and it was fun to figure out what the story was about. Each time an actor said a word that Tuyet recognized, she would repeat it: cat, cake, sneeze, doll. She loved that it was about a mom and a dad with a lot of kids, just like her family.

But on *The Brady Bunch*, all the children had white skin and round eyes.

After seeing the show for the first time, Tuyet hob-bled into the bathroom and balanced herself against the sink in front of the mirror. She tried to pull her eyes into a round shape with her fingers.

Lara pounded on the bathroom door. "Let me in."

Tuyet did not answer.

Lara pushed the door open. Tuyet quickly took her fingers away from her face, but her sister saw what she had been doing.

Lara stepped up onto the bathroom stool so that the reflection of her face was level with Tuyet's. She touched the image of Tuyet's left eye.

"Brown," she said.

Tuyet grinned. She placed one of her own fingers on the reflection of Lara's right eye. "Brown," she said.

Tuyet gazed at herself and her sister in the mirror.

Of Mom and Dad's four children, only one was white like on *The Brady Bunch*, and that was Beth. Mom and Dad said that Beth was "homemade."

Aaron had come from Vietnam just like Tuyet, and he'd been a Morris since he was a newborn baby.

Lara had also been a baby when she was adopted. She had been born in a place called Calcutta. Tuyet loved the warm richness of Lara's skin and the fact that her youngest sister's eyes were as deep and brown as her own and Aaron's, yet they were round like Beth's. They all looked different, but they were a family just the same.

Tuyet loved being a Morris.

## Chapter Seven

## Church

Usually on Sunday mornings, Mom went to church, and she took Beth, Lara, and Aaron with her. Before the surgery Tuyet had gone with them, but ever since her return from the hospital, she had been allowed to stay home with Dad, who was not a churchgoer. Tuyet looked forward to these times with her father. They would play, and later she would help him prepare Sunday brunch for the family.

But on the Sunday about a week before her cast was scheduled to come off, Mom told Tuyet to get dressed for church.

Tuyet looked from Mom to Dad in confusion. Why did she have to go to church and miss her special time with Dad? Didn't Mom realize how much Tuyet cherished Sunday mornings? And didn't Mom know how embarrassing it would be for Tuyet to have to maneuver across the church parking lot, up the steps, and down the aisle with her cast and crutches?

Mom put her hands on her hips. "Scoot, Tuyet," she said. "I don't want to be late."

Resigned, Tuyet hobbled to her bedroom. Mom had laid out a beautiful new pair of blue bell-bottomed pants, and a patterned pink and blue top. Tuyet wished she could wear a pretty dress like Beth's favorite red one, or Lara's shiny yellow one, but the new pants fit perfectly over her cast and wouldn't get in the way of her crutches. As she buttoned up her new blouse, she smiled to herself. She would miss spending the morning with Dad, but it was a treat to wear such beautiful clothes.

She sat on the bed and pulled the red knitted slipper over the foot of her cast, then slipped her right foot into her shiny red shoe.

Dad waved good-bye as Mom hoisted Aaron onto her hip. She guided her three daughters out the front door and into the car.

Beth and Lara settled in the front seat with Aaron nestled between them. Tuyet slid into the back, sitting sideways so her knee was straight. Mom put Tuyet's crutches into the trunk, and got into the driver's seat.

When they arrived at the church, Mom circled the parking lot to look for a spot, but all the nearest ones were taken. Mom pulled close to the church entrance and rolled down her window.

Tuyet saw a familiar woman at the bottom of the church steps.

"Pam!" called Mom.

The woman turned. She waved to Mom. Then her face broke into a huge grin when she saw Tuyet through the back window.

Tuyet waved back. She knew Mrs. MacDonald well. On the very first Sunday that Tuyet had gone to church, she had been embarrassed, so afraid that people would stare at her. But it had been a wonderful experience. And after the service, Mrs. MacDonald had given Tuyet a doll—her precious Holly Hobbie.

Mrs. MacDonald gathered Aaron into her arms and Mom took Tuyet's crutches from the trunk. She held them in place while Tuyet slid out the back door and pulled herself into a standing position. Beth and Lara scrambled out the front seat.

"Thank you, Pam," said Mom, getting back into the car.

Tuyet watched as Mom zoomed away to find a parking spot.

Tuyet took one step forward on her crutches and nearly lost her balance when the tip of her left crutch landed on a stone.

Mrs. MacDonald's eyes widened in alarm. "Let me carry you in," she said.

Tuyet shook her head.

Beth explained, "Tuyet likes to do things by herself."

Mrs. MacDonald kept pace with Tuyet, taking one slow step at a time along with her. By the time they got to the top step, Mom had joined them, breathless from hurrying. Mrs. MacDonald passed Aaron over to Mom, and she went on ahead with the other children to find a pew.

Tuyet could feel the sweat break out across her brow as she stepped in through the entryway of the church. Was it her imagination, or had everyone turned to stare at her as she slowly made her way down the center aisle? With every step she took, Tuyet's face burned with embarrassment. She kept her eyes to the ground, placing her crutches carefully so she wouldn't trip.

When she was halfway up the aisle, Tuyet paused for a moment to see where her sisters were sitting. As she surveyed the congregation, she realized that people were not staring at her. Most had their heads bowed in prayer. The few who were turned toward her smiled in encouragement. Tuyet breathed in deeply and let it out again. It would all be okay.

When she finally got to the pew where Mom was settling Beth, Lara, and Aaron, Tuyet hesitated. The pew was too narrow for her to get into with her crutches — and even if she managed that, what about her cast? It came to just below her knee, so she could bend her leg to sit, but only for short periods, because after that, the weight of the cast made her knee ache.

Mom looked from Tuyet to the pew and saw the problem. She slipped out of her spot and found the minister. He brought out a small chair and sat it at the end of the pew. Tuyet sat down with relief, grateful to stretch her leg out in front of her, but she could almost feel the stares of the congregation at the back of her head. Again she wondered why Mom had made her come to church. Couldn't she have waited one more week?

But then the singing started. Tuyet closed her eyes

and listened. She didn't know the words or these particular songs, but the strong voices rising up together filled her with joy. At the orphanage in Saigon, whenever the nuns sang or led the children in song, the sounds of war were drowned out and forgotten, if only for a few moments. Here, the songs were different, but the effect was the same. Tuyet felt safe and wrapped in love.

It was hard with her crutches, but Tuyet was glad that Mom had brought her here.

## Chapter Eight

## June 8, 1975

Much as Tuyet loved listening to the music, going to church in her cast had been an exhausting experience. By the time they returned home, Tuyet was grumpy. She wanted nothing more than to go inside, flop down on her daybed, and take a nap.

Mom parked the car in the driveway, and Beth and Lara ran inside giggling, not waiting for Tuyet or Mom and Aaron. Tuyet became even grumpier.

Mom held Aaron on her hip and opened the car door for Tuyet, and then she held the front door of the house as Tuyet limped in. Every bone in Tuyet's body ached.

But when she stepped into the living room, she saw bright balloons bobbing on ribbons. She remembered the four balloons that Dad had brought to the hospital and she no longer felt tired. Balloons meant fun.

In the kitchen, Dad was holding a big plate with something that looked like a cake. But Tuyet's heart clutched with fear. The cake was on fire!

Mom and Dad and Lara and Beth all shouted together, "Surprise! Happy Birthday!"

They were grinning and giggling, but Tuyet was confused.

"Fire!" she said, pointing to the cake. "Bad."

Dad put the cake down on the kitchen table. The fire was coming from flaming sticks that had been pushed into the cake, and they continued to burn. Didn't Mom and Dad know how dangerous fire was? Someone had to put that fire out!

Tuyet hobbled to the sink, grabbed a glass from the draining tray, and filled it with water. She turned to the cake and was about to dump the water on it—when Mom grabbed the glass from her just in time.

"It's okay, Tuyet," she said soothingly.

Tuyet slumped down into a chair, mesmerized by the sight of the burning cake. This must be another strange Canadian custom—buying balloons and burning cakes.

"Blow out the candles," said Beth, dancing in one spot with the excitement of it all.

Tuyet shook her head, confused.

"I'll show you," said Beth. She leaned in until her face was just inches from the fire. Tuyet was frozen in fear for her sister. Why didn't Mom or Dad pull her away?

Beth took in a deep breath. Her lips formed a tiny O. Then she blew out, hard. One of the fire sticks stopped burning.

Beth pointed to Tuyet, and then she pointed to the cake.

Tuyet understood at last. It was her job to put out the fires. She stood up and filled her lungs with air. She blew with every bit of breath she had. The fire sticks went out. She slumped back down into her chair.

Beth grabbed Lara's hand and they both got up from the kitchen table and darted down the hallway. They came back moments later, each holding a brightly colored box tied with ribbon.

Lara thrust hers into Tuyet's hands. "Open mine first."

Tuyet understood; the pretty box was a present. She held it in both hands and bowed her head. "Thank you."

Chapter Eight — June 8, 1975

"Open," said Lara.

Tuyet stared at her sister, mystified.

Lara took the present back. "Like this," she said and she ripped the colorful paper.

Tuyet gasped. Why was Lara ruining the pretty box? Would Dad and Mom get mad at her? But when Tuyet looked across the table, she saw that her parents were still smiling. This was surely the strangest Canadian custom of all, ripping up little boxes.

Lara thrust the half-opened present back into Tuyet's hands, and Tuyet pulled off the rest of the paper to reveal a plain box. She opened it. Inside were small hard candies in a rainbow of colors. Tuyet set the box down on the table.

Mom shook her head. "Present," she said, pointing at the box of candies. "For you," she added, resting a finger on Tuyet's chest. "All for you."

Tuyet was stunned. The box of candy was for her? But why?

Beth set her box in front of Tuyet. "Open it," she said, her voice trembling with excitement. "I hope you like it."

Tuyet ripped the patterned paper off the second box.

Inside was a bright pink hairbrush along with a matching set of barrettes.

She grinned and turned to her sister. "Thank you, Beth."

Beth clapped her hands. "I am so happy that you like it."

Lara and Beth each brought over another box, and another. Tuyet opened them all. It hardly mattered what was inside, it was just so much fun, ripping the paper and opening the boxes. What made Tuyet happiest was seeing the joy on her parents' faces as she and her sisters and brother giggled.

When she was finished, Dad served brunch, and then Mom cut each of them a slice of cake.

That night in bed, Tuyet hugged Holly Hobbie tight and thought about the wonderful day she'd had: the balloons, the colorful boxes, the fiery cake—Lara and Beth's excitement.

Tuyet still had no idea what a birthday was, but it had been the best day ever.

## Chapter Nine

## Can you walk, Tuyet?

When they pushed open the door to the Fracture Clinic at McMaster Hospital, Tuyet was astonished to see so many adults and children with casts—on their legs, feet, wrists, and arms. She and Dad found the only two empty chairs that were next to each other in the crowded room, so Tuyet sat in one of them and propped her crutches in front of the other to save it for Dad while he checked in at reception.

They waited for what seemed like hours, but Tuyet didn't mind. She watched the other people in the room and tried to imagine why they had cemented body parts. Maybe some of them had fallen and broken their bones. Maybe some had polio like she did. It was amazing that bones could be fixed this way, by putting them in cement for weeks and weeks.

A white-uniformed woman came into the waiting room and looked down at the clipboard she was holding. "Tuyet Morris?"

Dad held her crutches upright and Tuyet stood. They followed the nurse into a small room with a cot, a desk, a chair against the wall, and a stool on sliding castors. The nurse pointed to the cot and said to Tuyet, "That's for you."

Tuyet sat on the side of the cot and Dad helped her swing her legs up onto it, then he pulled off her red slipper. They were barely settled when a man came in holding a mean-looking instrument with a long electrical cord and sharp metal teeth.

He plugged in the instrument, sat down on the stool, and pulled up close to Tuyet's cot. He smiled and said, "This won't touch your skin. It's only to open the cast."

Tuyet didn't understand. She looked over at her father.

"It will be okay," he said gently.

The man flipped a switch on the instrument. It made a loud, grinding buzz.

Tuyet's heart pounded. Surely he wasn't going to use

that electric saw to remove the cement? What if it cut all the way down to her leg? She gripped the sides of her cot.

He brought the saw to her leg.

Tuyet's father gave her a nod of encouragement, and she held her breath. She could feel her entire leg vibrating and the buzz became a high-pitched whirr.

Under her breath, she chanted, "Please don't cut my leg open, please don't cut my leg…"

She wanted to close her eyes, to make it all go away, but that was impossible. She was paralyzed by the sight of the whirring saw teeth making a clean, grooved line down the entire length of her cast. When he got to the bottom, he took a pair of snub-nosed clippers and snipped through the bottom edge of her cast. Then he rolled his stool in closer and carefully snipped the top edge of her cast.

He motioned for her to flip over and he repeated the same exercise on the back of her cast. Dad helped her get into a sitting position when the man had finished grinding. Tuyet watched the man spread open her cast with a thing that looked like salad tongs. Beneath the cast, her leg was wrapped in white cloth. The man snipped some more—then the cloth and cast were off her leg.

## Chapter Nine—Can you walk, Tuyet?

Tuyet looked down at her leg and gasped. Bits of white fluff and plaster still clung to her skin, but her leg was perfect and straight. Her foot wasn't curled under her ankle anymore and the calluses were gone. Tuyet put her two legs side by side. The left one was still about six inches shorter than the right, but it was straight. She wiggled her toes and grinned.

Out of Dad's pocket came the red slipper. Tuyet pulled it over her tiny perfect left foot.

Would she be able to walk on it like this? Tuyet didn't know.

Tuyet was used to the weight of her cast, so using the crutches without the cast made her feel out of balance.

They didn't go straight home after leaving the fracture clinic. Dad parked on the street in front of a corner store. Why were they shopping now? Tuyet was anxious to get home so she could show Mom her perfect foot and her straight ankle.

There was quite a bit of traffic on the road, so Dad stood protectively by the passenger door while Tuyet got out. He held her steady as she hopped beside him to the trunk of the car to get her crutches.

They walked into the store together.

It was packed with all shapes and sizes of crutches, wheelchairs, canes, and scooters. Some of the crutches and canes hung from the ceiling on hooks and others hung from racks on the walls. The wheelchairs were collapsed and stacked against one of the walls, and the shelves and bins were filled with all sorts of parts, bolts, and fasteners. Tuyet had to maneuver carefully with her crutches so she wouldn't knock anything over.

Tuyet watched Dad walk up to a friendly-looking man with glasses poised on the tip of his nose. They exchanged a few words, and then the man walked over to where Tuyet stood.

"I'm Joe," he said. His eyes looked kind as he peered at Tuyet over his glasses. Then he looked down at her foot. "Let's measure you for a brace."

He motioned her to balance on a platform and he measured the dimensions of her left leg. Then he measured the length of her right leg for comparison. He also measured both feet.

"Come back in two weeks," he said.

Tuyet was anxious to show off her perfect foot to her family, but it had been such an exhausting day. By the time they pulled into the driveway, her eyes were beginning to droop.

Dad offered to carry her inside, but Tuyet didn't want Mom to think there was something wrong. After all, this was her first day with a straight foot. Shouldn't she be able to get around better than when she had the cement on her leg?

It took less strength for her to hobble with her crutches now that the cast was gone, but she felt out of balance. By the time she got to the front door and up the stairs to the living room, her back was aching.

Mom, Lara, Beth, and Aaron crowded around, grinning with excitement.

"I want to see your new foot," said Beth.

Tuyet hopped over to the daybed and sank into it with a grateful sigh. Aaron toddled up to her and pulled at her red slipper. Tuyet smiled. Even Aaron was excited to see her perfect foot. She helped him tug the slipper off then held up her foot for everyone to see.

Lara clapped her hands. "It is beautiful," she said.

Mom sat down on the daybed and handed Tuyet a gift-wrapped box. It wasn't her birthday, but it was a special occasion. Tuyet tore off the paper with glee.

Inside was a single red shoe. It was exactly the same as the one she wore on her right foot, only smaller. Tuyet slipped her perfect new foot into the shoe.

She hugged Mom and admired her feet. She couldn't remember ever wearing a pair of shoes that matched.

# Chapter Ten

# Strength

While Tuyet waited for her brace to be made, Dad took her to a place called a physiotherapy clinic. It was something like a hospital, except that she didn't have to stay overnight or have her leg cut open. But like a hospital, the therapists were dressed in white and they looked after patients who had weak arms or legs.

One of the walls was covered from floor to ceiling with a mirror; the other walls had cheerful wallpaper with tiny flowers. A woman was soaking her arm in a swirling tub of water. A man sat in a chair while a physiotherapist guided one of his feet into a vat of hot liquid. The man pulled his foot out and Tuyet stared in amazement as it started to cool. His foot was completely enclosed in wax!

Tuyet wondered if her own foot would be plunged in swirling water or hot wax. She wouldn't mind that. It looked almost like fun. But a white-coated woman led her instead to a parallel set of railings that faced the mirror. Dad held onto her crutches and the woman motioned for Tuyet to hold onto one end and to walk toward the mirror.

As the woman chatted away to her, Tuyet wished more than ever that she could speak English. Couldn't the physiotherapist see that she wasn't able to walk without her crutches? How was she supposed to hold onto the railings and get to the end with only one foot on the ground? But the woman smiled and motioned for her to move forward.

Tuyet felt the coolness of the wood as she wrapped the fingers of her left hand around the left railing. Then she gripped the right railing with her other hand. Using the full strength of both her arms, she lifted her body up and hopped forward one step.

The woman motioned with her hands for Tuyet to keep moving.

"You can do it, my dear," said Dad.

Tuyet looked up at him. He smiled. That gave her

strength. Tuyet looked at the reflection of her two legs. The one that did all the work, and the other one that hung uselessly. This woman had a reason for making her do this odd walk. Tuyet hopped again with a combination of arm strength and determination. And again. One step at a time, she got all the way to the mirror.

Thank goodness it was over. Sweat rolled into her eyes.

But the woman was not finished. She led Tuyet over to a chair and motioned for her to sit. Then she pulled up another chair and sat beside Tuyet. The woman planted her two feet on the floor in front of her. She placed something floppy covered with flowery cotton on one of her own ankles. Slowly, she raised her ankle until her knee was straight.

"Now, your turn," she said, giving the floppy thing to Tuyet and pointing to her left ankle.

Tuyet was surprised by how heavy the thing was. It seemed to be filled with sand. She placed the odd sandbag on her own small ankle. Frowning with effort, she slowly lifted the bag until her knee was straight. The physiotherapist made her do this exercise so many times that Tuyet's leg began to feel like rubber.

The woman handed the sandbag to Dad. "She needs to do this exercise at home each day."

The physiotherapist then lifted Tuyet onto a high table and had her lie flat on her back. She straightened Tuyet's leg, then put one hand on her kneecap and pushed down. She placed her other hand on the sole of Tuyet's foot and pushed firmly toward Tuyet's knee.

"Try to push your foot into my hand," said the woman.

From her hand motions, Tuyet realized what the woman wanted her to do, but it felt so uncomfortable. Even when Tuyet didn't push back, the pressure from the woman's hand pressing down on her knee was almost unbearable. But when Tuyet did push back, the pain was even worse.

But Tuyet tried not to think about all of that. Instead, she remembered what Mrs. Nguyen had told her. All these things they were doing to her leg were to help her to walk. Tuyet gulped in a lungful of air and then pushed hard with her foot.

"Good work," the physiotherapist said. "Now you are done for the day."

\* \* \*

Each day Tuyet worked until she was exhausted. At the end of each session, all she wanted to do was go home, curl up on the sofa, and watch *The Brady Bunch*. But each day before she went home, a physiotherapist would bend and push her foot and ankle. Her weak leg would ache and tingle from the treatment, and Tuyet wished that she didn't have to do it, but she could feel her leg getting stronger. Tuyet began to dream of a time when she might walk without crutches.

10-1

*An updated version of the leather and metal brace that Tuyet wore.*

After two weeks of physiotherapy, Dad took Tuyet back to Joe's store. He had a leg brace built just for her. The brace was made up of a parallel set of metal rods that started above Tuyet's knee and attached to a platform under her foot. The rods were straight above and below the knee, but right at the knee they each had a joint so they could bend with her. The whole device was held together with leather straps.

Joe helped strap Tuyet into the leg brace. The bulk of it made her weak leg almost as wide as her good leg, but her foot did not touch the ground. Tuyet wondered how she was supposed to walk in this thing.

Joe held up one finger and said, "I'll be right back." Then he walked down the hallway and stepped into a room at the end. Moments later he came back, holding a shoebox. He set it in front of Tuyet and removed the lid.

Tuyet was shocked by what she saw. Inside the box was the ugliest pair of shoes she had ever seen. They were brown and looked like men's shoes. One was flat, and the other had a sole built up six inches.

10-2                   *A pair of orthopedic shoes*
*similar to Tuyet's*

Tuyet removed her beautiful red shoe from her good foot. She slipped on the ugly flat brown shoe, and Dad helped her lace it up. Next, she slipped off the small red shoe from her left foot. She slipped the built-up shoe over the brace and over the tiny foot. Dad helped her lace that one up too.

Tuyet looked down. The right shoe was so ugly compared to her beautiful red shoe, but it wasn't nearly as ugly as the huge built-up brown shoe that she had to wear on her left foot. Tuyet thought she would weep from the sheer ugliness of her footwear.

But she didn't.

Instead, Tuyet surprised herself by smiling.

"It fits well," said Joe. He unlaced the shoe and slipped it off, then unbuckled the brace.

Tuyet sat down and Dad slipped her red shoes back onto her feet. She frowned in confusion. Wasn't she going to be wearing the brace and the ugly shoes from now on? But Dad pointed at what Joe was doing.

Joe removed the insert from the built-up shoe and squeezed gel inside. He fitted the base of the brace inside the shoe and put the insert back in, pressing down firmly so the gluey gel connected the shoe and the brace together.

"In one week, the gel will set and your brace will be ready," said Joe.

The week ticked by slowly. Much as Tuyet loved her shiny red shoes, she looked forward to having two feet on the ground. When they finally stepped into the store a week later, she was beside herself with excitement.

Joe greeted them with a smile. He brought out her brace with the shoe attached and, with careful precision, showed Tuyet how to put it on. What had been gel now felt solid under the insert. Once the brace was done up and both shoes laced, Joe got her to walk with her crutches and the brace from one end of the store to the other. He made some tiny adjustments, then asked her to walk again. Once more, he made an adjustment.

Finally, he was satisfied.

Tuyet bowed her head. "Thank you, Mr. Joe," she said carefully.

She grinned broadly as she and Dad walked out of the store together. Maybe the shoes were ugly, but they got the job done. For the first time in her memory, both feet were solidly on the ground at the same time.

# Chapter Eleven

## One Step At A Time

Tuyet used the crutches to get back to the car, and she unlocked the knee joints on the brace so she could sit. The leather and metal dug into her thigh, but she was determined to get used to the brace.

Tuyet looked out the window as Dad drove back to Brantford. They had been back and forth from Hamilton to Brantford so many times that the half-hour trip had become a routine. Dad would chat with her in English, and she would try to figure out what he was saying. Sometimes it was easy; she learned the words for colors and vehicles. But other times she had no idea what he was talking about. She smiled at him and nodded whether she could understand or not. Tuyet loved the sound of Dad's voice almost as much as she found comfort in his snores at night.

Tuyet's mind filled with thoughts about how much her life had changed in the past few months. She wondered what she'd be doing right now if she hadn't been rescued. Would she have stayed in the orphanage with the nuns—the only child left? Or would soldiers have found her? The last image she had of Saigon was a city filled with soldiers and tanks, and people running away in fear.

She looked out Dad's side window and saw the steep granite wall of Hamilton Mountain. She turned her head and looked out her own window. From where they were on the highway, she could see down the mountain and a vast area of houses. She wondered if any of the children who had been with her in the rescue from Saigon now lived in those houses. Tuyet thought of Linh, the older girl she had met on the airlift. Linh had visited her a few times and Tuyet had been ecstatic. She hoped they would see each other again, but Linh never came back. The disappearance of Linh was just one of many losses she had endured. Most of the time she tried not to think of bad things, but sometimes she couldn't help it.

Dad reached out and squeezed her hand. Tuyet's eyes filled with tears of gratitude. Even though they didn't speak the same language, Dad always understood what she was thinking.

Tuyet looked down at the way her braced left leg bulked out under her bell-bottoms. What a smart tool the brace was. To think that people could make a leg work, first by dipping it in cement, and then wrapping it up in leather and metal. She felt through her pant leg to find the metal joints at her knee, then with both hands she straightened her leg out slightly so it was more comfortable. It would take getting used to, wearing this brace, but she was determined to make it work.

Before she knew it, they were home.

Dad parked the car in the driveway and pulled Tuyet's crutches out of the trunk. He walked around to the passenger side, but he knew better than to try to help Tuyet out. Instead, he smiled, holding her crutches, and waited for her to get out on her own.

Tuyet swiveled in the seat so that both of her ugly brown shoes rested on the driveway. She pulled herself to a standing position by holding onto the car door, then pushed the knee hinges on the brace so that her left leg was straight and the hinges locked in place.

Tuyet held onto the crutches. The new sensation of wearing the brace made Tuyet feel out of balance, but she took a deep breath and stepped forward with the built-up shoe. So far so good.

With Dad by her side, Tuyet stepped slowly to the front door. It took strength and willpower and concentration, but Tuyet was determined to do it on her own. When she got through the front door to the inside steps, she was thankful that she had done all those physiotherapy exercises. Would she have been able to climb the steps on her own if she hadn't strengthened her leg? Probably not.

Tuyet kept the shoes and brace on. She wanted to practice walking around the house. She used the walls for balance and practiced maneuvering around toys and furniture.

When it was time to go to bed, Mom helped her take the brace off. Her skin had red rub marks where the straps had been buckled, and her leg felt tingly from the exertion.

"You are doing so well with your brace," said Mom as she gently massaged lotion into the sore spots on Tuyet's leg.

Tuyet felt heavy with exhaustion. She got into her pajamas and fell asleep quickly. Until—

She was jolted awake in the middle of the night. She sat up in bed and looked over at her ugly brown shoes, one with the brace sticking out of it. They sat neatly at the baseboard beside her crutches. She got out of bed and picked up the plain brown shoe that she wore on her right foot. With the help of her crutches, she carried the brown shoe out to the living room and down the six steps to the front entrance. She gazed at the row of her family's shoes in the moonlight. Six pairs were lined up—one pair for each family member. Tuyet's big and little red shoes sat between Beth and Lara's shoes. She took her red shoes out of the row and replaced them with the one brown shoe.

Tuyet leaned back on her crutches to admire the row of shoes. The red shoes were pretty, but they were only for show. The brown shoes would help her walk.

When she fell back to sleep, she dreamed of standing upright without holding onto crutches. She dreamed of walking on her own.

# Chapter Twelve
# The Hardest Things

The time before she came to Canada seemed like a distant nightmare as the days lengthened into summer and the sun warmed Tuyet's face. In July, Dad set up a wading pool in the backyard and filled it with icy water.

Tuyet loved playing in the pool on the hot summer days with Beth, Lara and Aaron. She didn't need her brace, and the cool water soothed her muscles and skin. Sometimes cousins would visit; other times, family friends would bring their children to splash and play with the Morris children. Tuyet loved playing, and she loved being surrounded by so many children.

But Tuyet especially loved holding Baby Aaron on her lap. She showed him the blades of grass and how to make them whistle, just as Dad had shown her on her first days in Brantford. She loved breathing in the scent of Aaron's downy hair and feeling the warmth of his chubby body as she wrapped her arms around him.

But holding Aaron made her heart ache with a loss that had no words. Wisps of memory would come back, of another boy, long ago. A boy who may have been her brother. She hugged Aaron tight and whispered in his ear, "I love you, dear brother. Don't ever leave me."

Once, when she, Beth, and Lara were building a giant castle in the sandbox, Tuyet heard an ominous sound from above. Through the clouds she saw the silhouette of an airplane. A stream of pale dust was falling from the belly of the aircraft.

"Run!" Tuyet screamed. She grabbed Beth's hand and pulled her up. Then she scrabbled over to Lara and Aaron. "Inside, inside!"

Tuyet crawled toward the kitchen door, pushing and pulling Beth and Lara and Aaron as she went. "Not safe!" she cried.

Mom opened the sliding door and stepped outside.

"Inside!" cried Tuyet, pointing to the sky. "Not safe!"

Mom looked up to the sky and saw the silhouette of a crop duster. She pointed. "Is that what's not safe?" she asked Tuyet.

Tuyet nodded. Bad things came out of airplanes. Bombs, poison, fire.

Mom picked up Tuyet and hugged her fiercely. "You are safe, my dear daughter. The airplane is dropping seeds, not bombs."

Tuyet didn't understand the words, but she could tell that Mom was not frightened. As she melted into her mother's reassuring embrace, she closed her eyes and tried to block her fear.

Mrs. Nguyen explained to Tuyet that when September came, she would go to school. "You will learn English there," she said. "And there will be lots of children like you. Children who speak languages other than English."

"Will any of them be on crutches?" asked Tuyet.

"I don't know," said Mrs. Nguyen. "But not all hurts show on the outside."

Tuyet nodded. This she understood.

\* \* \*

12-1    *Tuyet ready for school, holding
her Holly Hobbie doll.*

Tuyet continued to go to physiotherapy. At the clinic she would do exercises without her brace, then put the brace on and do some more. She would watch herself in the mirror as she carefully stepped forward, wearing her brace and built-up shoe, but without holding onto her crutches. At first she could barely take a single step forward, but with patience and practice she gradually improved.

The hardest thing was to walk outside without the crutches. Lawns were uneven, and so were driveways and sidewalks. But that was another skill for Tuyet to practice. She would walk without her crutches close to the wall of the house or the wooden back porch, so if she lost her balance, she'd have something to hold on to.

One day, at the end of the summer, Tuyet walked all the way down to the end of her driveway without crutches. Her back ached and her face was red from the exertion, but she did it. And it felt exhilarating.

She stood in front of her house and surveyed the street. This was the first time she had stood here on her own—on her own two feet.

Just then, she heard running footsteps from next door followed by a *thump* and a *whoosh*. A soccer ball bounded along the neighbor's lawn and rolled until it stopped just in front of her.

Tuyet looked up and saw the boys who lived next door. The younger one began to run toward the ball, but Tuyet held up her hand.

She carefully lifted her right foot until all her weight had shifted to her new perfect foot and the built-up shoe.

## Chapter Twelve—The Hardest Things

Then, with her other foot, she kicked the ball firmly, right back to them.

# Historical Note

Polio is an abbreviation for poliomyelitis, a virus that can be spread through contaminated food and water. Children are more often infected than adults.

When a person first contracts polio, they may have no symptoms at all, or perhaps a mild fever. Most people recover without long-lasting damage, but one in a hundred will have permanent paralysis, because the virus affects the central nervous system and destroys the nerve cells that make muscles work.

If a child's leg is damaged by polio, it stops growing and stops building muscle. The undamaged leg keeps on growing. This means that by the time a child becomes an adult, one leg could be six or eight inches longer than the other. And the short leg and foot will be weak and thin.

Polio can also stop the muscles in the foot and ankle from developing. When this happens, the damaged foot may turn inward. This is what happened to Tuyet. While she was at the orphanage, Tuyet taught herself to walk by putting all her weight on her anklebone or the side of her heel.

When a person walks on the side of their foot, they do even more damage to their ankle. Their posture is no longer straight, which can cause other health problems as well as pain.

Surgery to straighten the ankle makes it possible for a shoe and brace to be fitted, and this corrects posture so it no longer hurts to walk and other health problems do not develop. Best of all, it means the person will be able to walk on the sole of their foot instead of their ankle.

Up until the 1950s, polio was the most feared disease in North America. Thousands of children and adults had their arms, legs, and respiration permanently damaged because of polio. In 1955, the Salk vaccine was introduced, and the widespread use of the vaccine curtailed the spread of this terrible disease in North America. In 1962, the Sabin oral vaccine was introduced. It wasn't until the mid-1970s that Canada had polio under control. The US was declared polio-free in 1979. Canada was certified polio-free in 1994.

While North America is polio-free, the world is not so fortunate. In countries suffering from poverty or war, polio can still run rampant. The World Health Organization and the Centers for Disease Control and Prevention consider the eradication of polio to be a top world health priority. These organizations, along with UNICEF and Rotary International, have been working for decades toward the eradication of polio worldwide. Over the years,

Rotary International volunteers and fundraisers around the world have helped immunize more than two billion children against polio. Since that time, the incidence of polio has declined by 99%. As long as one person is still infected, however, we are all at risk for its spread.

# Further Resources for Parents and Teachers

## Internet

- Would you like to help make the world polio-free? Contact your local Rotary Club.
  **The Rotary Foundation of Canada:** www.trfcanada.org
  **Rotary International:** www.rotary.org

- *Joint initiative with Rotary, UNICEF, WHO, and the CDC:*
  **Polio Global Eradication Initiative:**
  www.polioeradication.org

## Books

- *In the Clear*, by Anne Laurel Carter, Orca Book Publishers, 2001

- *Dear Canada: To Stand On My Own: The Polio Epidemic Diary of Noreen Robertson, Saskatoon, Saskatchewan, 1937*, by Barbara Haworth-Attard, Scholastic Canada, 2010

- *Small Steps: The Year I Got Polio* (Anniversary Edition), by Peg Kehret, Albert Whitman & Company, 2000

# Author's Note

This first surgery to straighten Tuyet's ankle was just one of six corrective procedures that Tuyet endured over the years. If she had not received these surgeries, she would never have been able to walk. Tuyet had her final set of surgeries just before starting high school. Her short leg was lengthened and her long leg was shortened.

Back in the 1970s, parents were not allowed to stay with their children in the hospital. And back then, there were no services in place for patients who did not speak English. If Tuyet were a child now, the experience would not have been so terrifying.

Tuyet's actual birthday was on August 6th, not June 8th. Her mother and father had misread her Vietnamese birth certificate, which had listed her birthday as 06/08/1967. So on August 6th, she received a second birthday cake.

Although Mrs. Nguyen and Hoang Tuy (Tuy is his first name) are real people, their names are inventions. Tuyet still has gaps in her childhood memories, but she will never forget the kindness of these two individuals. Linh, Tuyet's friend from *Last Airlift*, is also real. Her name has been changed to protect her privacy. After she arrived in Canada and was adopted, it was determined that she was not an orphan at all, but the daughter of diplomats. She was reunited with her parents and moved to the United States. Tuyet never heard from her again.

I would like to thank Dr. William Vivianni, Tuyet's orthopedic surgeon, for sharing his insight; and Joe Cottone of C&DC Orthopaedic Services, who has known Tuyet since she was a child and has been providing her with shoes and braces for all these decades.

Tuyet's sisters, Beth and Lara, were generous and helpful with their time and memories. Thank you, Beth, for connecting me with McMaster Archivist Anne McKeage, who not only guided me through the photography archives of McMaster University Medical Centre, but took me on a tour of where Tuyet had stayed while at the hospital. Anne also kindly read this manuscript.

Dorothy Morris, as always, you are wonderful.

Special thanks to Gail Winskill: I would not have written nonfiction without your encouragement.

Ann Featherstone: thank you again for helping me make the words shine.

I am in awe of Tuyet's incredible determination and

her strength of character. Thank you, Tuyet, for allow-
ing me to share your story.

15-1

*The Morris children in 1976.*
*Front, from left, Beth, Aaron*
*and Lara. Behind, Tuyet.*

**Marsha Forchuk Skrypuch** managed to hide the fact that she couldn't read until grade four, when she failed the provincial reading exam. Too proud to ask for help, she taught herself how to read by taking out the fattest book she could find in the children's section of the Brantford Public Library, *The Adventures of Oliver Twist* by Charles Dickens. She had to renew the book for a whole year, but she not only managed to finish it, she learned to love books. Reading that big, fat novel, she says, was a turning point in her life.

Today, Marsha is the author of more than a dozen historical picture books, chapter books, and juvenile and young adult novels. She has received numerous awards and nominations for her work. Her most recent children's book, *Making Bombs For Hitler*, is the companion novel to *Stolen Child*, which is a MYRCA Honor Book, an OLA Best Bet, a CLA Book of the Year nominee, a Diamond Willow selection, a Resource Links Best Book, a Golden Oak selection, a CCBC starred selection, and the SCBWI Crystal Kite winner for the Americas.

In 2008, in recognition of her outstanding achievement in the development of the culture of Ukraine, Marsha was awarded the Order of Princess Olha, which was bestowed upon her personally by President Victor Yushchenko. Marsha lives in Brantford, Ontario.

Tuyet would like to add her thanks.

To my dear husband, Darren: you are my rock.
And to my precious kids, Luke and Bria:
you fill my heart with joy.

# Index